THESES ON REPEALING EXORCISM

composed by Dr. Aegidius Hunnius shortly before his departure from this life so that they might be publicly discussed in the Academy of Wittenberg.

Erfurt ✦ Martin Wittel ✦ 1606

translated by Rev. Paul A. Rydecki

edited by Rachel Melvin

Foreword by Rt. Rev. James D. Heiser

REPRISTINATION PRESS
MALONE, TEXAS
2013

Published in 2013

REPRISTINATION PRESS
P.O. BOX 173
BYNUM, TEXAS 76631

www.repristinationpress.com

ISBN 1-891469-53-3

FOREWORD

The history of the rite of exorcism in connection with the Sacrament of holy Baptism is sufficiently obscure within the modern Evangelical Lutheran Church that is seems likely that few American Lutherans are even aware that many of the churches of the Augsburg Confession retained that rite for generations after the beginning of the Reformation. For those who are familiar with Luther's decision to retain exorcism in his 1526 revision of the Order for Baptism, a few words from Dr. Robert Kolb neatly summarize what is often repeated concerning the decision to retain or remove the exorcism during the later phase of the Reformation:

Exorcism as a component of baptism proved to be the most controversial aspect of the rite during this period, one that offers insight into the way the laity understood the sacrament. Luther included the practice in his *Taufbüchlein* of 1526, but many (including Luther himself) considered it *adiaphoron*, and most of the Protestant churches of southwestern Germany excluded the rite. However, its strong rejection by the Calvinists led some territories to retain it, in order to demonstrate their Lutheran orthodoxy.[1]

However, while it is certainly possible that such geographical proximity to Calvinist centers could have influenced some city or territorial churches regarding the decision to retain or omit exorcism, Hunnius' *Theses on Repealing Exorcism* offers an opportunity to reevaluate the difficulties associated with such a sweeping assertion.

---

1   Robert Kolb, *Lutheran Ecclesiastical Culture 1550–1675*, (Brill, 2008), p. 279.

Hunnius was a member of the theological faculty of the University of Wittenberg from 1592 until his death in 1603. According to Schmeling, the exorcism was restored to the Order of Baptism in Saxony in that same year as part of a campaign to remove the pernicious influence of crypto-Calvinism, and the Visitation Articles which were adopted in Saxony in 1592 had Hunnius as their "chief author".[2] Therefore, it would seem reasonable to conclude that Hunnius supported the restoration of exorcism in 1592 as an item of anti-Calvinist polemic. However, by the time of his death in 1603, Hunnius had come to see exorcism in a different light. It is quite telling that those Reformation-era theologians whom Hunnius cites as supporters of exorcism were men who had opposed adoption of the *Book of Concord* (1580) as the definitive statement of Biblical, Lutheran doctrine. From Hunnius' perspective, an adiaphoristic rite which aided the Lutheran confession in 1592 was no longer viewed in such benign terms a decade later.

It has become increasingly common for Luther's *Taufbüchlein* to be restored in Confessional Lutheran churches in North America, and the reappearance of Luther's 'lesser exorcism' has attended the reappearance of that Order of Baptism. As Confessional Lutherans consider the restoration or retention of the 'lesser exorcism,' they would do well to consider Hunnius' *Theses*, and evaluate their validity in our own circumstances.

Rt. Rev. James D. Heiser
Monday of Oculi, A.D. 2013

---

2   Gaylin R. Schmeling, *Polykarp Leyser (1552–1610): A Theological Bridge Between Chemnitz and Gerhard*, p. 5 (Accessed online at http://www.blts.edu/wp-content/uploads/2011/06/GRS-Leyser.pdf)

THESES ON EXORCISM

Thesis 1

Baptism as instituted by Christ consists of the element of water and the Word of institution, that is, the Word of promise, so that the one to be baptized is sprinkled with water in the name of the Father and of the Son and of the Holy Spirit for the remission of sins, regeneration, and the sealing of the adoption acquired by Christ.

Thesis 2

Nothing beyond this pertains to the essence of Baptism, nor to its effects. Rather it should either be included among the Adiaphora, or it should be removed as a weed that was not planted by God—if, that is, it is either wicked in and of itself, or if it leads to wickedness because it is thought of as worship or as necessary.

Thesis 3

Exorcism is to command Satan to depart from an infant and to make room for the Holy Spirit. Furthermore, it is to tell an infant to receive the sign of the holy cross on † the forehead and on † the breast. Finally, Satan is solemnly commanded to depart and withdraw from this slave and bondservant of Jesus Christ.

6

Thesis 4

In addition, these things are done without adding any sort of statement that would remove the idea of a corporeal possession of the infant, or that would mitigate the superstitious understanding of necessity or of worship. Nor is it affirmed that the power of Satan is destroyed and the liberation of the infant is secured, not in the act itself of Exorcism (as indeed the words manifestly claim for themselves), but only in Baptism, when the infant is washed with water in the Name of the most holy Trinity.

Thesis 5

Therefore, with regard to this ceremony of Exorcism, the question is whether or not, in the words noted above and in the accompanying gestures, the practice is entirely consistent with the Holy Scriptures.

Thesis 6

Furthermore, I do not wish to press the point here that the word itself, which is unknown to the uneducated, if it is put into our language, means, "a conjuring of the devil,"[3] a word that, although it is softened in translation, already seems to insinuate something blasphemous, seeing that long ago the gift of the miraculous casting out of demons from the possessed ceased. Today we know of no other Exorcists, except for the sacrificing priests of the Pope and those who either command or disown Satan with magical incantations.

---

3   *Teuffelsbeschwerung*

Thesis 7

Dr. Chemnitz writes the following concerning this matter in the second part of his *Examination of the Council of Trent: Afterwards, although that gift (of casting out Satan) had ceased, so that the order of Exorcists might be retained, another duty was invented for them to perform, namely, that they might prepare the catechumens who were to be baptized for Baptism by means of Exorcisms and exsufflations, as the book* Concerning the Doctrines of the Church, *ch. 51, testifies. And Gregory of Nazianzus says: "Do not be dismayed with the rather long training of Exorcism, and do not grow weary on account of its length." But such a peculiar rationale for Exorcism did not exist in the Apostolic Church, nor was this the duty of the Exorcists of the ancient Church, neither is it now observed even among the papists, etc."* Thus far Dr. Chemnitz.

Thesis 8

An example of this is seen in 1 The. 5: "I charge[4] you by God that this Epistle be read to all the brothers." This does not pertain at all to the matter at hand, since Paul is charging Christians, not Satan, and especially since he is not making the sign of the cross as is done when the names of the Persons of the Trinity are recited in the rite of Exorcism. Nor is it at all helpful to imitate, even in appearance, the same manner (if one observes the outward form) in which the sacrificing priests and others used to do with their magical incantations, as the passage says, "Abstain from every appearance of evil,"[5] especially because this rite of exorcizing in the name † of the Father and † of the Son and † of the

---

4   Latin: *adjuro*
5   1 The. 5:22

Holy Spirit has neither the foundation of Scripture nor the example of practice in the Apostolic Church.

Thesis 9

Furthermore, the question isn't whether Exorcism, in the papistic sense, should be understood according to the Scriptures, for who could assert such a thing except for the papist himself? But must be understood from the sense that is customary in our churches.

Thesis 10

Therefore, one must distinguish between the sound of the words themselves and the explanation of them that has customarily been given by several people in the Lutheran churches.

Thesis 11

This is well and good, but it misses the point. For surely the form of the words is never entirely devoid of its context. Of this there can hardly be any doubt.

Thesis 12

To be sure, not even in the Lutheran churches does everyone share the same opinion or conclusion concerning Exorcism.

Thesis 13

Indeed, on the one hand, some can be found who state that Exorcism is necessary, and that without it, the integrity of Baptism is not entirely certain.

Thesis 14

The Smalcaldic pastor, Master Alexander Uzinger, refers to a certain pastor in the province of Hennenberg who baptized an infant without using the rite of Exorcism. Then not long afterwards the infant fell out of its crib. The men of that region blamed it on the omission of the rite of Exorcism. So the parents asked the pastor either to baptize the child again with the rite of Exorcism being followed this time, or at least to perform the rite of Exorcism.

Thesis 15

He tells of another example in addition to this. A certain infant had been baptized in the case of necessity, without the rite of Exorcism. When, after several days, it seemed that the child was about to die, the parents brought the child to the pastor again and begged for him to perform the rite of Exorcism on the child. I myself can attest that a certain distinguished woman affirmed to trustworthy persons that she believes that her little daughter who is about 11 years old has become much less submissive, because, when the Calvinists were in charge, Exorcism was not performed on her. What? Can it be that some necessity is attached to Exorcism—as if Baptism by itself were less efficacious if the rite of Exorcism is removed from it?

Thesis 16

There is no doubt that this idea of necessity has firmly set in among the common people, as also the excited mobs demonstrate if at any time its abolition is feared, so that they fight for it no differently than they fight for their pews or some other aspect of worship.

Thesis 17

Thus it is well-known to the chief theologians who advocate for Exorcism that some degree of superstition and error adhered to it, as long as they judged that an infant was prepared in some way by the act of Exorcism so that he was thereby able to be admitted to Baptism more worthily.

Thesis 18

In the same way, even the rite itself seems to indicate this. For the infant is not brought immediately to the baptistery, but is sent ahead to some other place for the ritual of his Exorcism. Once this is done, only then is he considered to be fit to come into the baptistery so that the other act can be performed on him.

Thesis 19

Nor should one imagine that this notion has set in only for the commoners, but certainly also for the most learned. This is demonstrated by examples that clearly show that those very men ascribe to the act of Exorcism the divine power to cast Satan out of infants.

Thesis 20

Dr. Tilemann Heshusius[6] says this in a letter to a certain doctor of theology, among others: *I cannot see that Exorcism serves any other purpose than to destroy Satan's kingdom and to rescue the little child out of his slavery.*

Thesis 21

Likewise, in another letter written in the year 1562, there is another page that says: *I see that Cyprian, Optatus Milevitanus, Gregory Nazianzus, Iactantius, Augustine and other outstanding teachers of the Church not only think highly of Exorcism, but also ascribe great power to the office of the Holy Spirit. Augustine says in* De Nupt. et Concu., *Book 7. ch. 20: "The demonic power is real and is not cast out of the children in vain through the conjuring[7]. And since the children cannot do it for themselves, those who bring them to Baptism must with their own heart and mouth renounce the devil on their behalf, in order that they may be rescued from the power of darkness and brought into the kingdom of God."*

---

6   Tilemann Heshusius (1527–1588) earned his doctorate at Wittenberg in 1533, was Superintendent of Goslar and deposed in 1556. He was a professor at Heidelberg, but lated deposed, then Superintendent of Magdeburg, until being deposed. Later he was again deposed and exiled by crypto-Calvinists in 1573, and served as bishop of Samland in Koenigsberg until he was deposed in 1577. Finally, he served as a professor at Helmstedt, where he helped prevent Brunswick from accepting the Formula of Concord.

7   *beschweren*

Thesis 22

And again on page 134: *If anyone should wonder by what authority the Church and the Ministers of the Word presume to have the right and power to drive the devil out of the child and undertake to disrupt the devil's tyranny through Exorcism and conjuring, he should know that the Son of God has granted this authority to the Church. Indeed, this is a special gift that has been bestowed, that Christ has given the Apostles the authority to drive out demons in His name.*

Thesis 23

Page 367: *And that already in those days there was, together with the dispensing of Baptism, a formerly received and active use and ceremony—yes* (to use Augustine's words), *an ancient ecclesiastical tradition (Book 2.,* De Nup. et Con.*) to drive out the devil through Exorcism—that is evident from the rulings of the bishops who consulted together at the Council of Carthage.*

Thesis 24

In addition, he alleges and approves on page 8 the conclusion of Optatius Milevitanus, Book 4, who says: *For no one is unaware of the fact that everyone who is born, even if he is born to Christian parents, can never be free of the spirit of this world, whom one must first drive out of a man and banish before the cleansing of Holy Baptism. This is accomplished through Exorcism, by which the unclean spirit is driven out and chased away into the wasteland.*

Thesis 25

Thus also Dr. Jacobus Colerus[8], in his book on Exorcism from 1588, page 5, approves and cites in Latin the saying of Bishop Optatius Milevitanus: *It escapes no one that every man who is born, even if he is born of Christian parents, cannot be without the spirit of the world, who must be cast out and banished from the man before the salutary washing. Exorcism serves this purpose, through which the unclean spirit is driven out and forced to flee to deserted places.*

Thesis 26

Dr. Colerus also approves of this, to such an extent that he produces for his *Institutes* this conclusion of Isidorus as confirmation of his own conclusion: *This is why children are exorcised, so that, after the devil leaves them, they may safely come to Baptism.*

Thesis 27

In these examples, that which was supposed to be attributed only to Baptism is being attributed to the act of Exorcism itself, especially if, as the words say, Satan is cast out of the infant through Exorcism before the salutary washing, so that, after the devil has left him, he may safely come to Baptism. It is almost like the manner in which the power to forgive sins used to be attributed to the papistic Sacrament

---

8   Colerus (1537–1612) was Professor of Hebrew, Frankfurt (1576–1577), Provost at St. Nicolai in Berlin (1577–99), Superintendent at Güstrow in Mecklenburg (1599–1612)

of Confirmation, which follows Baptism. A man was thought to be fortified against Satan through confirmation, with this formula: *I mark you with the sign of the holy cross † and I confirm you with the anointing of salvation in the name of the Father and of the Son and of the Holy Spirit. Amen.*

Thesis 28

In this way, therefore, it is established that Exorcism is a part of worship and, in the words of Heshusius, *the Ministry of the Holy Spirit through which God works that purging.*

Thesis 29

But if Exorcism is to have the power and ability to cast out Satan, then this power must come from a command and promise. But where is the word and promise? And if such a command exists, then won't Exorcism have to be removed from the list of Adiaphora and added to the things that are necessary?

Thesis 30

Since it is supposed to be a part of worship, and infants cannot go without it, and the Churches sin that do away with it, then surely the Apostles themselves sinned when they failed to include Exorcism in the act of Baptism!

Thesis 31

Indeed, isn't it true that in this way, as much efficacy will be lost from the Baptism instituted by God, as is attributed to the Exorcism instituted by man?

Thesis 32

Therefore, when Exorcism is understood in this way, it plainly pertains to human traditions, by which the Lord testifies that He is worshiped in vain (Isa. 20, Mat. 15). In this regard there is a memorable sentence in the written account of the recusal of the Electors and Princes, where they give their reasons for refusing to attend the Council of Trent. This is how the words read, page 204, Silver Edition: *The Holy Scriptures testify that Christ commanded Baptism in the name of the Father and of the Son and of the Holy Spirit, and that He commanded neither anointing nor Exorcism to be performed (Mat. 28). Therefore, these two practices are not of Christ, but are human institutions, and therefore belong to those things of which Christ said in Matthew 15, "In vain do they worship Me with things commanded by men."*[9]

Thesis 33

If, by this mistaken notion, someone in the hour of death places his confidence for salvation and liberation from the devil partly in Baptism and also partly in Exorcism, doesn't he go dangerously astray? I leave the matter to the judgment of all who judge rightly.

---

9   Quotation in German.

Thesis 34

Indeed, this is why I am not very surprised that in a certain famous place two years ago, a writing was published by us in which this superstition is confirmed by example. I refer to these words:

Thesis 35

The story is told of a great prince who was greatly tormented by the evil foe through all kinds of evil spirits. And it so happened that once, when he witnessed a Baptism and also heard the word of Exorcism, he asked the priest whether he also had been baptized in this way. The priest answered, "Yes." Then the prince replied, "Ah, well then, I will no longer worry about the devil; he has no power over me."

Thesis 36

But it is as if, had he been baptized without Exorcism, he couldn't have taken as much comfort in his Baptism. This also I should wish that you would observe, not only that the sound of the words of Exorcism seems to indicate to the unlearned a corporeal possession, but that this notion is confirmed by the booklets of certain people that have been written concerning Exorcism. Even if the suspicion of this error should be removed from these booklets, certain words of theirs would still seem to be inclined to it.

Thesis 37

Justus Menius[10] says this, among other things: *All Christian preachers who baptize with sincerity and devotion will see and discover that, when the word of Exorcism is spoken, such gestures are made that can be seen and heard on and in the child.* The matter itself testifies how closely these things approach the description of the man who is corporeally possessed.

Thesis 38

Many things here are objectionable. There are those who point out that the outward form or manner of speaking sounds overly harsh, while the substance, that is, the doctrine, remains sound. But I reply: the Holy Spirit does not only insist that the substance or doctrine be sound, but also that the pattern or the form of the words be preserved (2 Tim. 1).

Thesis 39

But you may say: The goal of Exorcism is not that by these words ("I command you to depart") and in that act Satan should be driven away and the child freed from him. I reply: Why, then, does Exorcism promise this very thing, both with words and with voice and also with this gesture, to those who are gathered around? For neither the form of the

---

10   Justus Menius (1499–1558), served as Superintendent at Eisenach and Gotha. Noted as an opponent of Osiander, but was apparently an adherent of the party of Georg Major (1502–1574), which taught the "necessity" of good works for salvation—a teaching which was denounced in the Formula of Concord.

words nor the manner of the action expresses or represents anything different.

Thesis 40

You insist that the sense of this formula and action is not what takes place in the Exorcism but what God is about to do in the divinely instituted act of Baptism that follows.

Thesis 41

I reply: That is well and good. But in this way, the Minister is saying one thing, while something else is to be understood by the hearers. Indeed, what Sibyl[11] could possibly guess this sense from the words? Neither Peter nor Paul could understand these mysteries without the aid of an interpreter.

Thesis 42

In fact, the matter itself declares that this interpretation is not being deduced from the words, but is being imported into them and forced upon them. We have, to this day, repudiated this violent and preposterous manner of interpretation in our adversaries when it comes to controversial questions.

---

11   A prophetess from Greek mythology.

Thesis 43

Others may reply that it is a sort of prayer that God would mercifully deliver the child through Baptism out of Satan's kingdom, where it is held captive.

Thesis 44

But, in the first place, the same response can be given here that was added to the previous declaration; for who could possibly guess that this is a form of prayer? For indeed, in prayer a dialogue is initiated with God; it is Him we address, not Satan. All the faithful have prayed against Satan since the world was formed, and a very many forms of prayer are read everywhere throughout the Scriptures. But that any of the faithful has ever prayed in this way to any Person of the Trinity, by giving Satan a command and making the sign of the cross—that is not read or found anywhere.

Thesis 45

Indeed, what in the end could be so absurd, so abhorrent to the ears and hearts of the pious? There is no excuse for these kinds of contrived interpretations.

Thesis 46

Thus a Christian who is about to go out, perhaps into a severe storm, or even walking in the dead of night, says: "I command you, unclean spirit, in the name † of the Father and † of the Son and † of the Holy Spirit, not to bring me any injury, but that all your power to harm should be thoroughly impeded."

Thesis 47

Thus, about to get out of bed, in the place of his customary prayer, he says: "I command you, unclean spirit, not to be able to harm me this day in any way."

Thesis 48

Likewise, as he is about to have breakfast, he will command him in the name of the adorable Trinity not to bring any harm through food or drink (as he may often do with God's permission), just as they long ago used to safeguard themselves under the Papacy against the perils of storms or dog bites or encounters with wolves.

Thesis 49

These and many other things could be defended by the plausible interpretation that they are nothing other than forms of prayer, for it is established from the Scriptures that the devil is the "prince of the air," and rules over the darkness of this world, shoots his flaming arrows in the darkness and lays traps in every way possible to jeopardize the safety of men. Therefore the Christian man, to whom authority has been given in a spiritual manner to trample upon every power of the enemy, in this way vanquishes his authority, lest he should be able to tempt him without regard to any permission of God.

Thesis 50

I shall offer one additional example. A certain man is about to enter the temple in order to hear a sermon. In the place of prayer he will begin with auspices the Exorcism in this way: *I exorcise you, unclean spirit, in the name of the Father, etc., that you should depart from me, lest you should overturn the fruitfulness of the divine Word within me.* If someone who is standing close by hears this and nudges the Exorcist with his elbow, asking what on earth he is doing, won't he naturally reply that he is praying? For since Christ testifies that Satan is present when the Word is preached and gives heed to intercept the scattered seed so that it may not bear fruit, therefore he is driving him away with this form of prayer! For why is it not permissible to him to fight against Satan in this way, since authority has been given by God to any Christian to conquer the devil by faith and prayer?

Thesis 51

But the right response, both here and in the question of Exorcism, is that nowhere does there exist a command or an example in the Holy Scriptures that such forms are to be used, that it is permissible to use even the name of God against Satan in this unusual fashion. But we are commanded in the Scriptures to use forms that have a clear and immovable foundation in the Word of God.

Thesis 52

For if not even Michael the archangel, who constantly struggles with the devil, dares to smite him with a curse, as the Epistle of Jude says, or to go against him on his [angelic] authority, then surely for the same reason we are not permitted by human authority to fight against Satan with any forms whatsoever. No, it is certainly only appropriate to follow the safe manner which we see expressed in God's Word, lest, by that dialogue that has been initiated and by that harsh signing of the cross and by the solemn use of the divine name in a matter that is insufficiently clear, something should be committed by which either the name of God is profaned or by which the broad road is paved that leads to superstitions.

Thesis 53

And indeed, since God has commanded by a special precept, "You shall not take the name of the Lord your God in vain, etc.," it should certainly not be used, especially with so much solemnity, except in matters which we know for certain from the Word of God, either as precepts or certainly as things that are lawful. Otherwise the invocation of the divine name cannot be done from faith. For faith comes from the Word of God (Rom. 14). But whatever does not come from faith is sin (Rom. 14).

Thesis 54

As long, then, as it cannot be acceptably demonstrated that this rite is in agreement with the Word of God, but is only performed for long-held but poor reasons, just so long is faith also weakened, and consequently in that unusual commanding, it does not appear that the name of Father, Son and Holy Spirit can be used properly.

Thesis 55

How is it that the name of the glorious Trinity is used with greater solemnity and with more gestures in the rite of Exorcism than in the words of Baptism, where certainly the Father, Son and Holy Spirit are named—but without regard to the sign of the cross, and rightly so.

Thesis 56

But since the unlearned commoners and the vast majority of people have their eyes fixed on the external rites and gestures, there is no doubt that this is why it happens that the rougher crowd in whom that notion about the dignity of Exorcism has become firmly rooted, and often times they pursue the act of Exorcism with greater devotion and reverence than the act of Baptism, and they are confirmed in this conclusion by the solemnity of the ceremonies. Sensible men easily understand how preposterous this is.

Thesis 57

You may say: "Nevertheless, if Exorcism should be adequately explained to the people, there would be no danger." I reply: "And when, exactly, is it explained? Indeed, how many times does the opportunity present itself in a year? And why is the Church wearied with a rite of this kind that requires such a tedious explanation that doesn't accomplish anything at all unless it is repeatedly impressed and forced upon the common people?"

Thesis 58

We see that only with much labor can the necessary articles of faith, even the most familiar ones, be impressed upon the simple commoners. How, then, shall we inculcate this hidden sense of the words of Exorcism?

Thesis 59

There may certainly be some who will grasp it; but there will also be many who will not grasp it. This would certainly be discovered if each one separately were to respond to this question and if the thoughts of their hearts were to be expressed.

Thesis 60

What is more, who are they who ought to explain the true sense to the common people? Naturally, it would be the pastors. But how few of the pastors thoroughly and rightly comprehend this business, since it is well-known from the aforementioned examples that the most learned among them talk idly in this matter?

Thesis 61

You continue to plead your case: "There is great usefulness in Exorcism, for those ceremonies make a confession concerning original sin, concerning the captivity of infants in Satan's kingdom, and also concerning their beneficent liberation through Christ, and that against the Pelagian notions of the Anabaptists and Sacramentarians."

Thesis 62

Does this make any sense? Isn't it rather the case that these articles can be declared much more properly, vigorously and clearly in some forms in common use that come from the Holy Spirit Himself with words drawn from the Scriptures? And can't the magnitude of original sin, the misery of the little ones and the benefits of Christ also be set forth without the spectacle of Exorcism? This could well be done with greater usefulness and with less danger in many parishes.

Thesis 63

Therefore, since this information can be conveyed in a manner like this that neither causes anyone any scruples of conscience nor supplies an occasion for superstition, nor is there a constant dispute with regard to origin and substance, what need is there for Exorcism, which is dangerous for so many reasons? Would it not have been better to omit that which is so tedious to explain, or when not explained and repeatedly inculcated, is a most definite source of perverse superstitions?

Thesis 64

This is so true that the esteemed Dr. Chemnitz admits that *the Church is not bound to that prescribed rite of Exorcism, but has the freedom to set forth and explain that doctrine* (concerning original sin, the authority and kingdom of Satan and the efficacy of Baptism) *with other words that are MORE compatible* (he says) *with the Scriptures.* When he says "more compatible with the Scriptures," he is clearly testifying that the rite of Exorcism is less compatible with the Scriptures.

Thesis 65

This, too, is one of the reasons why all the godly should wish that Exorcism had been repealed long ago, or that it still might be repealed, lest there constantly be new commotions to dread because of it:

Thesis 66

It is well-known that if Exorcism should be even lightly tampered with and not treated with a most tender hand, then immediately new disputes will arise—not only disputes of the Calvinists against us, but also of us against one another.

Thesis 67

This is just what happened in the year 1551 with the Goths among the Ministers of their Church at the time of Justus Menius. It happened again in the year 1562, but also around the year 1584 among the Ministers of the Hennebergian Church, as well as ten years prior to that in this Electorate by the Calvinists.

Thesis 68

Therefore, the legitimate repeal of Exorcism can be considered also for the tranquility of the Churches in the future, as all prudent men understand.

Thesis 69

In addition, this would serve for conformity among the Churches. If this were to be instituted, no sane person could deny that those Churches that have been using Exorcism up till now would yield to the Churches in which it has been absent. For even today those Churches that withdraw from the Papacy also remove Exorcism together with the rest of the superfluous ceremonies. Indeed, in this way one more closely approximates that Apostolic simplicity employed in Baptism. And Dr. Chemnitz, in the words cited above, and Dr. Selnecker, in Part 4 of his *Theological Examination*, writes that *in those Churches where the use of Exorcism is absent, it should not readily be reinstituted.*

Thesis 70

Indeed, even that excessive praiser of Exorcism, Dr. Heshusius, says in a letter written in 1583: *I think even more highly of the Apostolic simplicity than of all the pomp of ceremonies.*

Thesis 71

Here you will loudly object: "If Exorcism is to be repealed on account of the continual disputes that are stirred up, then for the same reason the very doctrine of the Gospel would have to be repealed, since not fewer disputes tend also to arise on its account, as Christ testifies in Matthew 18."

Thesis 72

But there is an enormous difference. The doctrine of the Gospel rests on the expressed Word and commandment of God, and therefore it is to be set forth, even if earth and hell be ruined. Exorcism, however, is nothing but a human tradition that can be abolished without harm to godliness, lest the Church be damaged so often because of it.

Thesis 73

But certainly someone will complain to me that this cannot be done without disturbing consciences. What is this I hear? Are you talking about the consciences that have been bound to superstitious notions regarding the necessity of Exorcism and other things, or are you speaking about the consciences that have been properly established by the Word of God?

Thesis 74

The latter cannot be disturbed by the known reasons for repealing Exorcism, for they know that it is a human ceremony and that the declaration that is ascribed to it can much more readily be replaced by a clearer form that is more consonant with the Scriptures.

Thesis 75

But as far as the former are concerned, far from being left behind in the realm of superstition, they should rather be taught the necessary information concerning this very issue and removed at length [from their superstitions] by the legitimate rationale behind the rite of Exorcism, in order that those depraved notions may be banished from the minds of men.

Thesis 76

Now if we should consider its first origin, it is clear that Christ never instituted it, nor did the Apostles employ it in the act of Baptism. Hence it lacks any word, and, consequently, if the notion of necessity comes up (which can happen all too easily and is certainly the case with innumerable people), the superstition has already produced a great deal of danger.

Thesis 77

Moreover, it was certainly instituted by the Church on good counsel, but it has not turned out to our advantage. Indeed, it may be that in the minds of those who first invented it, it was not introduced for ill purposes.

Thesis 78

But even this is uncertain, since all of the most noble fathers who, in my findings, are cited in this question, attribute the power for casting the Devil out of the infant entirely to Exorcism, even before the child is washed with the water of Baptism in the name of the Father and of the Son and of the Holy Spirit.

Thesis 79

The sayings of Bishop Optatus Milevitanus and of Isidorus cited above teach this all too clearly.

Thesis 80

Cyprian, in his *Letter to Januarius*, very clearly seems to approve of those papistic ceremonies, most notably in that he thinks it is necessary for the water to be purified and sanctified first by the priest in order for it to be able, by Baptism, to wash away the sins of the man who is being baptized.

Thesis 81

Likewise, it is necessary to be anointed, since he who is baptized can, once he has received Christening, be anointed of God and have the grace of God in himself.

Thesis 82

Basil, in his book *On the Holy Spirit*, ch. 27, ascribes those ceremonies to the tradition of the Apostles, namely, the Consecration of the water of Baptism and of the oil of anointing and of the one who receives Baptism, as well as that very anointing with oil.

Thesis 83

Augustine himself surely does not teach any more purely regarding these ceremonies that have to do with Exorcism. These are his words from his book *On the Doctrine of the Church,* ch. 31: *When either children or youth come to the washing of regeneration, let them not approach the font of life before the unclean spirit is driven away from them by the Exorcisms and exsufflations of the clerics.*

Thesis 84

There is a double error here. First, that no distinction is made between the infants and between the young catechumens, although it is certainly true that the catechumens had already been freed from Satan through instruction and knowledge of the Evangelical doctrine, so that it is absurd and a dreadful thing to command Satan "in the name † of the Father, etc.," to depart from a man who had already been rescued from the power of darkness through true faith, and about whom it cannot truly be said that he is possessed either corporeally or spiritually.

Thesis 85

The other error is that Augustine asserts that they are not to be admitted to the font of life before the unclean spirit is driven away from them by the Exorcisms and exsufflations of the clerics.

Thesis 86

Our churches judge the opposite to be true. Rather than teaching that an infant should not be brought to the very washing of regeneration before Satan is driven away from them through Exorcism, they more correctly declare that Satan is not expelled from the infant by Exorcism or by any other means than by Baptism, as all Scripture testifies.

Thesis 87

Indeed, if that notion of the fathers should hold sway, then wouldn't those infants who have not been exorcized come to Baptism more impure than those who have been exorcized? And thus something of divine efficacy would be affixed to a human ceremony.

Thesis 88

Thus also Augustine wrote and judged even less properly regarding the exsufflations that were connected with Exorcism, saying in Book 2 of *De Nup. et concupis.*, ch. 18: *Thus (Pelagius) accuses the Church as it has spread throughout the world in which and wherein all the infants who are to be baptized are not exsufflated for any other reason except that the prince of this world may be driven out of them.* He repeats the same thing in Book 6, ch. 2, *Against Julianus.*

Thesis 89

From these things it is clear that not even the beginnings of Exorcism were entirely pure, and that not even the fathers who were most trustworthy in other respects were free from all corruption in this case. What, I ask, will become of the common people? Surely they will never be so well instructed that no superstition is to be feared among them, especially with words that are so suspect, so given to inciting superstition according to their native sense.

Thesis 90

So then, even the argument that is deduced from antiquity will not avail, because we have demonstrated that Exorcism included something of a perverse notion from its very first origin.

Thesis 91

To be sure, this rule is firm: as soon as something besides the Word of God is affixed to a human rite, it immediately degenerates into superstition, and as the Savior mentions with this unfavorable sentence: "Every plant, etc.," and "In vain do they worship Me" (Mat. 15).

Thesis 92

Nor is it that we are objecting to those sayings concerning the authority given to the Ministry. For that authority is limited by its boundaries, and God has expressed with a clear word what kind of authority it is and how it is to be exercised, namely, to "Preach the Gospel" (Mark 16), "Declare in My name repentance and the remission of sins among all nations" (Luke 24). And "whosoever sins you remit, they are remitted" (John 20). Likewise, "Baptize in the name of the Father and of the Son and of the Holy Spirit" (Mat. 24), and in the words of the Supper, "Do this." This command refers to the whole institution.

Thesis 93

This is that authority of the Ministry to which the Savior gave this boundary in Mat. 28, "Teach them to observe all things that I have commanded you." But Christ nowhere gave the order to perform Exorcism, or to command Satan—certainly not with the use of the name of the glorious Trinity.

Thesis 94

Certainly the sayings concerning the authority given over unclean spirits is asserted, but which of all of those sayings can finally be applied to the papistic rite of Exorcism?

Thesis 95

For either they are dealing with the expulsion of demons from those who are corporeally possessed, in which case nothing exists with regard to the institution; or they are speaking of spiritual authority to destroy Satan's rule. And if you are ascribing that authority to Exorcism, then are you not taking the power that belongs to Baptism and conferring it on a human ceremony?

Thesis 96

Certainly since God wants the authority attributed to the Ministry to be efficacious, which the very word "authority" indicates, come, then! Explain what that efficacy of Exorcism is! But it is certainly not possible to assign any efficacy to it. For we are not dealing with the efficacy of Baptism, which we know to depend on the authority of the Ministry. But we are asking only and distinctly about Exorcism.

Thesis 97

But if you should say that it does not for that reason refer to the authority of the Ministry, as if Exorcism itself had some sort of efficacy, but that it declares what God effects in Baptism, then you will already have been drawn back contrary to the institution to the judgment of those who state that the declaration is merely what God works, not through Exorcism, but through Baptism. And so all those things that were said above in Theses 41 and 42 already militate against this interpretation. We also wish for those things to be repeated here in this case.

Thesis 98

Add to this that the authority given to the Ministry is to be exercised for edification, according to that saying of the Apostle, "God has given me authority for building up, not for tearing down" (2 Cor. 13).

Thesis 99

But I leave it to all the godly to evaluate whether it serves for edification when a ceremony is tenaciously retained that, by the very sound of the words and by the very gestures involved, strews the way with perverse methods—a ceremony that has so often thrown the Church of God headlong into disputes which could have been avoided by using a different form that was more compatible with the Scriptures.

Thesis 100

But even the authority of Blessed Luther is used against us, and if indeed there are any who make much of this chosen instrument of God, I also include myself among them without hesitation.

Thesis 101

In the matter at hand, I reply honestly that it could have happened that, due to habit, Luther was less offended by this rite[12], and perhaps on account of the weak, he judged that it should be tolerated for a period of time.

12   *formula*

Thesis 102

Just as Philip Melanchthon says in his letter to the Transylvanians: *Even if there are some words in Exorcism and in the confession of faith over which some people would fight and quarrel, nevertheless they are not willing to cross swords with anyone, but they permit it on account of custom and on account of the weak.*

Thesis 103

The Apostles, too, tolerated a very many things on account of the weak, but only for a time. It is right, however, that the weak should finally also grow up into the measure of full stature of the adult Christ and not remain weak forever, so that eventually those things that had to be tolerated on their account can be legitimately removed.

Thesis 104

But to me, the custom of certain people is not at all approved who do not handle this in such a way that, beyond the usage that Exorcism (properly understood) can have, they do not at the same time demonstrate also the problems with it. Although the nature of the Office requires that they should fortify men against the perverse notions about Exorcism, they are entirely silent concerning the dangers and only praise the things that they think are praiseworthy in it, so that the notion that it must be retained becomes more and more firmly rooted, nor can the right moment ever arrive for repealing it.

Thesis 105

And certainly Exorcism was able to be retained without as much danger at the time of Luther, because at that time there were no disputes of this kind being raised over the matter of Exorcism, nor were the abuse or the sinister notion of Exorcism observed then as it is today.

Thesis 106

In addition, the doctrine of Luther is well-known that ceremonies that furnish the seeds of superstition must be removed in due course, to the extent that if even the bronze serpent that was lifted up in the desert and kept in the sanctuary should provide occasion for superstition, he confirms that it must be destroyed.

Thesis 107

But even the argument concerning the weak has its limits and, finally, its end, for it does not last forever, as the practice of the Apostles clearly demonstrates.

Thesis 108

And it is not the best proof, since, when God mercifully granted His Gospel to these lands 80 years ago, our men over such a long interval of time had not yet decided about the use of Adiaphora, which must undoubtedly be ascribed partly to ignorance and partly to the negligence of the pastors themselves.

Thesis 109

Even if it were right to wait so long while everyone is being properly informed, since the fact is that there are many among them who are not interested in any information and who have inquired little after the business of godliness, nothing in the Church could ever be emended.

Thesis 110

I am pleased with Luther's conclusion when he says: *We have enough Scriptures—reason teaches us what is harmful for salvation and what may be changed without sin— that one can calmly and securely change and remove unseen devils, the world, and all that belongs to them. For undoubtedly King Hezekiah must also have suffered very many wicked speeches from the godless when he disturbed their worship, as the Rabshakeh accused him, and especially when he ordered the holy, divine serpent to be broken in pieces. This must have made him tremble terribly—to assault this serpent, a divine work commanded by God's Word and long esteemed by many kings and prophets who were, to be sure, holier and more greatly enlightened than he may have been. The godless surely know how to grind and sharpen their speech as they cry, "Do you think that all the former teachers knew nothing? Do all of our fathers have to be fools in your eyes? Could it be that God allowed so many among His people to err?"—and many things like this, as our godless people also do at the present time. When they are unable to prevail any further against the truth and against the Scriptures, they say, "I want to remain with the old faith. Can it be that you alone see what no one else has seen?" But Hezekiah did not inquire about any of these things. He went ahead anyway, no matter who wanted him to allow the serpent idol to remain. Thus we do also. Whoever wants to keep the pope as an idol remains a pope-idolater. We wish, together with Hezekiah, to do away with every form of corruption, even if it should be a serpent of iron or gold that has been in existence for a long time. Christ alone must remain forever. May He be praised and blessed! Amen.*

Thesis 111

But neither am I satisfied with the speech of those who are offended by Exorcism and claim that it is not the ceremony, but the men themselves who are to blame.

Thesis 112

This might well be true, if it were a ceremony commanded by God (just as long ago [the fault] could not be ascribed to circumcision that people were offended by it), or if the sense of the words were more properly sound and approved.

Thesis 113

But now, since the rite itself in its genuine sense—which the sound of the words renders without any ambiguity and in which sense the fathers also understood it—thoroughly indicates that by means of Exorcism, Satan is expelled from infants before they come to the salutary font of Baptism (which we demonstrated above from Augustine, Optatius Milevitanus and Isidorus, not to mention Heshusius, Colerus and Justus Menius), therefore it does not work to attempt an escape by the manner of speech; Exorcism in and of itself offends the minds of men.

Thesis 114

Moreover, the sense with which it has now been dressed up by its more recent proponents is indeed sound, but it is novel, foreign and forced; it is neither found among the fathers, nor does it arise from the form of the rite, but is being read into it.

Thesis 115

Observing this uncomfortable truth, some of the noblest churches have judged that it should be entirely repealed so that they may prevent the occasion of offense and also look out for their men in the future.

Thesis 116

Thus those churches have already been freed from this concern and from this most troublesome declaration, and from the intensification of this declaration and from the fear of superstition among the simple, as also from the danger of disputes and from other difficulties which were mentioned earlier.

Thesis 117

Nor does it take anything away from those Churches, after they substituted in place of this unfortunate rite another rite that is skillfully expressed, clear, drawn from the foundations of the Holy Scriptures, and also easily understandable to the simple and free from all of those concerns and misfortunes.

Thesis 118

But someone may object that the Churches were not disturbed before Exorcism was opposed by restless men; that, if Exorcism were left intact, then the Church would have its tranquility completely unharmed.

Thesis 119

I am sure that is true! For since the people are immersed in superstitious notions and ascribe to Exorcism a certain special efficacy, it is true to such an extent that if this ulcer were to be touched even by sound theologians, the common people would not be able to bear such counselors but would defile them with curses.

Thesis 120

The pastors bear a good deal of responsibility in this matter, for even if they preach a great deal about Exorcism, all their speech still tends toward this, that they commend it among the people, but not so as to remove the depraved notions concerning it by pointing out the unfortunate aspects with which it is afflicted. In that regard they are more speechless than fish.

Thesis 121

This evil, however, is not averted by silence but by clearly indicating what the benefit can be when it is properly understood, and also what dangers it carries with it if its use is not most precisely understood. How difficult this is, there is no lack of examples, not only among the hearers but also among the pastors themselves, even doctors, whose job it is to guide others to the true knowledge, as with a kind of torch.

Thesis 122

Finally, something must also be said concerning the words, "Receive the sign of the holy cross † on the forehead and † on the breast."

Thesis 123

This ceremony, besides the inane gesticulation that meets the eyes, seems to have hardly any usefulness; and it involves things that likewise have the semblance of superstition.

Thesis 124

I do not wish to press the point here that the sacrificing priests use gesticulations of this kind in their religious
rites, for a similar rite is used in the Papistic Sacrament of
Confirmation when the priest says: *I mark you with the Sign
of the holy cross* †.

Thesis 125

I would like to know this: Why only on the forehead
and on the breast? Why isn't the whole infant signed with
a larger sign of the cross? What about the rest of the body?
What about the soul? Indeed, what, I ask, does that bare sign
accomplish or admonish, especially when it is not explained
to the people?

Thesis 126

I have seen some who, when a bright flash of lightning strikes during a severe storm, are accustomed to protect
their forehead and breast with the sign of the cross, as if they
were now safe against the lightning strikes and thunderbolts.

Thesis 127

Now, for my part, I would not have a problem if there
were no superstition involved; but the human soul, given as it is
to superstitions, can hardly contain itself from attributing some
sort of efficacy to the sign itself when it is made in this way.

Thesis 128

If the sign of the cross is supposed to serve as a reminder of the cross itself, that is, of the suffering of Christ that makes us secure against demonic assaults, then well and good. But why does the Minister not omit the sign and speak instead about the true cross and passion of Christ with clear words? Or if he really wants to show a sign, why does he not add an explanation, like, "May the cross and blood of Jesus Christ rescue you from all the violence of the evil foe"? Or why not omit this entirely and leave it all to the act of Baptism, where it is established that the infant is defended from the tyranny of the devil as he is sprinkled with the blood of the Son of God (through the washing of regeneration)? But enough of these things.

THE END

www.ingramcontent.com/pod-product-compliance
Lightning Source LLC
Chambersburg PA
CBHW071650040426
42452CB00009B/1827